HILLBILLY ARMORED, INC.

To Lindsey

Thank you for helping me
fight breast cancer.

Daniel R Poncince

4/1/16

HILLBILLY ARMORED, INC.

DANIEL R. PONCINIE

HILLBILLY ARMORED, INC.

Copyright © 2013 by Daniel R. Poncinie

ISBN: 978-0-615-83024-7

Printed in the United States of America

10 9 8 7 6 5 4 3 2   06 28 13

∞ This paper meets the requirements of ANSI/NISO Z 39.48-1992
(Permanence of paper)

I have tried to recreate events, locales and conversations from my memories of them. In order to maintain their anonymity in some instances I have changed the names of individuals and places, I may have changed some identifying characteristics and details such as physical properties, occupations and places of residence.

This book is not intended for impressionable kids.

A note from Daniel

The book is very disjointed. It skips around from one thing to another, in no real order. Its also very politically incorrect, so dont say I didnt tell anybody. I wrote this wild book, because its all true. I did change everybodys name, to protect their identities. I also wrote it to entertain everybody, who reads it, and so people will understand why we do the job, the way that we do it.

HILLBILLY ARMORED, INC.

PART I

Hillbilly Armored inc.

This book is dedicated
To my friends and family
who have no idea That
I'm writing it.

I'm on vacation light
now Sitting by The pool.

This book is about
driving armored Trucks and
over twenty years of
memories of driving Them.
IT all Started on 9/13/88,
when I got hired on
Friday The 13th. I Should
have known Something
was up! There probably

Should have been some kind
of sign or indication of what
was coming. Twenty plus
years of long, long, days and
short paychecks. Was it
worth it? I haven't decided
yet, but it's time to kill
some small flying bugs.
There are so many bugs here
That I can't hope to kill
them all so let's get on with
the book.
Years ago, (I don't know how
many.) There were two guys
on a truck, starting on a run.
The driver was a former
winn-dixie truck driver.

The messenger was a former
professional football player.
Now in the armored truck
business, the messenger is
the one who rides in the
back of the truck, and takes
money into and out of the
stops. The messenger knew the
run, but the driver didn't, because
he was just starting up in
driving armored trucks. Well,
the messenger told the driver
to get on I85 north, and he
would tell the driver where
to get off at. So the driver
got on I85 north and started
driving. Now fast forward
3 hours and the following

conversation took place. Keep
in mind now, the messenger
has done his paper work and
is now sound asleep, but wakes
up three hours later, wondering
where they are.
   At the beginning:
messenger: Do you know where
the next stop is?
Driver : no, but I used to drive
for winn-dixie.
messenger: Ok, take I 85 north
and I'll tell you when to get off.
Driver : ok.
      Three hours later
The driver is wondering when
to get off the interstate.

The messenger _finally_ wakes up.

messenger: Where are we?

Driver: Well, a while ago I saw a sign that said welcome to South Carolina.

messenger: South carolina, SOUTH CaroLina! Turn This Thing around!

They wound up six hours behind Schedule That day.

Years Later, I was driving a run that went waaaay South of Atlanta. I was driving over I75, when I saw (yes really) a great big hot dog

7

driving South on I75.
needless to say, I called it
in to dispatch.
me: Hey base!
Dispatch: Go ahead.
me: I think I need a vacation,
I'm not feeling very well.
Dispatch: why, what's wrong?
me: I just saw a great big
hot dog, running South on I75.
And it was keeping up with
the other traffic!
Dispatch: Did it have mustard
on it?
me: yeah!
Dispatch: Did it have ketchup on it?
me: yeah!
Dispatch: was it on a bun?

me : yeah!
Dispatch: keep driving, you're ok.

IT hasn't always been That
fun Though. On more Than one
occasion, I have been Lucky
enough To avoid a robbery
by as Little as 1 or 2 minutes,
after iT happened.
The Trucks a Long Time ago
used To Let a LoT of exhaust
into The front cab of the
Trucks. So After all these
years, of breathing iT, some
of The stuff I write might
Sound Strange. I have driven,
Through every kind of weather,
ThaT Georgia has To offer, and

Seen a lot of things (good, bad, & crazy!) happen. I have wondered (and I still do.) how I managed to do it for all this time. And I still don't know. So I just keep on driving armored trucks and hope something will make sense. People have cut me off, gotten mad at me, flipped the 'bird' at me, and among other things cussed at me. This is because, they don't understand the nature of the job I do. But they still do all of those things anyway. So I would like to say, please give us truck drivers a break.

Sometimes I have ridden
"Shotgun" in the literal sense.
And I still enjoy it when I
get the chance to do it.
People still ask if we have
any "free samples." I just
tell them "yeah, but I keep
them for myself." I have
picked up a few nicknames,
over the years. The ones
that come to mind are,
Shotgun, John wayne, Wyatt Earp,
quick draw, dead eye, Doc Holladay,
gun slinger, etc. I got the
name Shotgun, because when
I first started driving
armored trucks, I also guarded
the front door with an

empty Shotgun. I got the
other nicknames because of
The way I wear my gunbelt.
Down Low on the right side
Like the old gunfighters
used to. I even had a
mustache to complete The
Look. By now, you're more
Than Likely wondering which
company I'm driving for.
well, I Started with ~~XXX~~
~~XXX~~ Armored, and Then in
1997 iT became ~~XXXX~~ ~~XXX~~,
and Then almost ten years
Later iT became Just plain
~~XXX~~. Some foreign company
owns iT now.

On another run a long time
ago, (yeah, I still don't remember.)
we were going up to northwest
Georgia. The truck had a
CB radio in it and those were
some fun days. But on this
one day, the truck broke down
and overheated. There we
were sitting on I 75 South
waiting for the engine to
cool down so we could limp
it to a gas station for
some water. The CB was on
and somebody say's "Anybody
want that Armored Truck,
back there?" So we started
counting how many bullets and
shotgun shells we had.

As Luck would have it, we had enough bullets, shotgun shells, and guns. So the truck cooled down, we got the water, and went back to base. I have had a Lot happen when out on the road. Things Like flat tires, transmissions that quit, an engine that threw a rod through the side of the engine block, a power steering pump that quit, brakes that failed, A/C that quit in the middle of July, and other things that make it fun to be stuck in the middle of nowhere.

Heat & Bend
↓
X

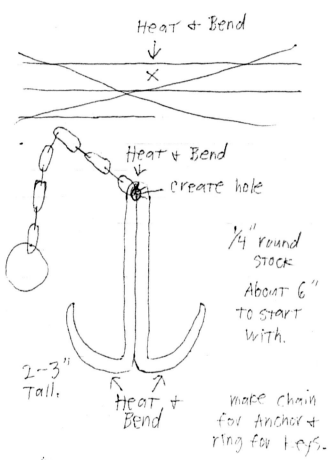

Heat & Bend
↓
→ create hole

¼" round
STOCK

About 6"
to start
With.

2--3"
Tall.

Heat &
Bend

make chain
for Anchor &
ring for keys.

¼" round Stock or Smaller Stock
or square   maybe ⅛" or ³⁄₁₆"

Put candle wax on it
for protection against rust
+ stamp ~~~~ ~~~ ~~~ D P
~~~~ " on it.
You'll have to forgive The
parts that are blocked out.
I did some editing. There's
some other things I just
remembered. One morning,
(around midnight) This guy
That worked in the vault,
got a phone call. His wife
wanted him to bring some
milk home for the baby.
So he left work, got some
milk, and took it home.
when he got home, his
wife Jumped out and

Stabbed him to death,
with a butcher knife.
He's buried in Texas, and
She's in Prison. Time for
a Change in Subject. Some
of the trucks we have are
at least over 20 years old.
Are you ready for This?
The Truck I'm sitting in
right now, has rust all
over the inside. With a
first Aid kit, that (and I'm
not kidding!) expired in
1999! This is being written
in September 2009. I have
to take a break now
because I'm getting
writers cramp.

The first aid box has
fallen apart from rust.
Believe me, The rest of the
truck isn't doing much better.
This thing dates back to
"Somewhere" in The 80's.
The windows have cracks
in Them, The tires are of
The "maypop" variety. It has
a Lift gate on The back,
that has seen better days.
In The front cab, (where The
alleged first Aid kit is)
we have A Braves Schedule
for The 2004 season. There's
The forgotten remains of
a shotgun rack, a "panic"
button, That probably is a

Sick Joke, and some other
Long forgotten Things That
I can't identify anymore.
The fuse box, is a Jumble
of black Lumps with a cover
That hangs on one hinge.
when This Thing Starts up,
it Sounds Like a
constipated turkey on crack.
There have been people
at work, That were my
friends, and they are no
Longer around. They died
from Things Like heart attack,
cancer, old age, etc, I won't
mention Their names, because
I want Their families To
have privacy.

The first I remember
is a woman who died from
cancer. She had blonde hair,
nice eyes, and was a really
good person to have as a
friend. She's in a better
place, but I still miss her.
Next is somebody who was
a WWII Navy veteran. He was
not afraid to say what he
thought about anything. But
everything he talked about,
or said had a "By God" in
it somewhere. I guess
that's just the way
he was "by god."

I need to put more detail
in this book, from now on
because until now, everything
has really been open ended &
vague. The "runs" that I
talk about, are simply a
list of places, that we
go to, during the day.
In the older trucks, the
windows in the rear half
of the truck, have what we
call "swiss cheese." This is
Just a thick plate of metal
with holes punched in it.
The holes are about the
size of a half dollar. The
newer trucks don't have it.

The older trucks also have chains welded to the doors. The "maypop" tires are just retreads. And they get their name from the fact that they may pop, because the tread separated from the casing. In the early 90's, I was on a run and the engine suddenly decided to throw a rod. We were just starting on the run, and as we were going up the interstate, the cab started filling up with smoke. So I told the messenger about it, and he asked me what was wrong. I said "Hell, I don't know! maybe it wants a smoke break."

So we got off the interstate,
at the next exit. The truck
went clattering down the exit
ramp, and we got stuck at a
red light. well, The morning
rush hour was in full swing, and
The truck died, There we were,
in a big red smoking dead truck,
with everybody staring at us.
I cranked the truck up, and
as the light turned green, we
clattered through the light
and into a parking lot, where
we called for help.

Nov. 2009. Here I (we) sit
somewhere in South Georgia,
broke down. The brake
system won't release the

electric parking brake.
So, we'll have to wait about
two hours to do a transfer.
The police car is sitting behind
the truck for security. The
sky is threatening to rain,
and I hope I don't have to
go shit! It's just a little
before 11:00, AM and this is one
hell of a day. We still have
about 99% of the run to do.
The branch down here is sending,
(I think anyway) a truck for us
to use. So while we wait,
I'll keep on writing this
book. There was somebody
else, that used to ride in the
truck with me.

I'm just going to call him
Red. one day, Red and I
were on a run that went
to the northwest side of
Atlanta. We had just started
using walkie-talkies on the
Truck so we could Let each
other know what was going
on at any given stop. Well,
at one stop, Red gets out of
The Truck, and walks up to
The door. He calls me on the
walkie talkie, and he's Laughing.
He says, "watch This! I'm
gonna go in here with a
hardon." Sure enough, he turns
sideways and from about a
hundred feet away, you could

See a big bulge in his pants.
About fifteen minutes Later,
he came back to the truck.
He said "Those women in There,
were Looking at me real funny,
and walking Sideways, with
Their backs to The wall." We had
a good Laugh about That, and
went on with The run.
On another run, we were down at
The Atlanta airport. It was in
The early 90's and The messenger,
Thought he was funny. He kept
Talking Like pee-wee Herman. He
also Looked Like he had a
2×4" Stuck up his ass. ~~~~~
~~~~~~
~~~~~~

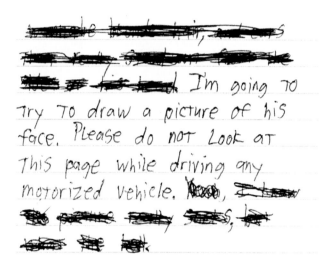 I'm going to try to draw a picture of his face. Please do not look at this page while driving any motorized vehicle.

Thanksgiving isn't far away, and thinking about that takes my mind off of waiting to switch trucks. It's 11:45 now and here we sit. The truck is supposed to be coming from Atlanta, but I don't know. We have just switched trucks, and here we go. The holidays have come & gone, and now it's 2010. So far, this year isn't too bad, but it could be better. I have to drive a run to Columbus tomorrow, and I don't know the whole run. The person riding with me, won't know it either, because he's

never been on This run before.
Tomorrow is going to be a
long day.

Fri. 1/29/10 That was a
long run! We didn't get done
until after 9:00 That night.
I'm scheduled to go to The
airport today. I'll be guarding
for somebody. There's a storm
coming into Atlanta This
evening, or Tonight. A few pages
ago, when we were waiting
to switch Trucks, there was
somebody That was riding with
me on The run. I'm going To
call him Zeb. We've been riding
on runs together over The years,

off & on. He was The union president for a Long Time. After Some years went by, he got tired of iT, and now we have a new union president.

2/18/10

What a night This is! I JusT got back from a run, and now I'm on a "Special", run. Two guys from AugusTa had Their Truck break down, and now we have To go To The Shop where They are, To help cuT Switching Trucks. So here we go. We geT To The Georgia World congress center, and all of a sudden,

There's a bunch of police, all over the place. And they're going towards northside drive. They have motorcycles, patrol cars, with lights on and sirens going. Now in the center of all of this, is a pickup truck hauling what looks like a cattle trailer. And the police are laughing. I can't imagine what the hell is so funny. We went to the place where the Augusta guys were, and switched the trucks, so they could get back to Augusta. On the way back to base, we found out what happened in downtown Atlanta with the police.

The circus is in town right
now, and a zebra escaped from
The circus. The Atlanta police
went after The roaming zebra,
and caught it. I can Just
imagine The charges against This
animal. 1. Escaping from The circus.
2. Evading The police.
3. Resisting arrest.
4. Disrupting Traffic.
5. Jay walking.
6. indecent exposure.
7. Disrespect for the Law.
8. Being an illegal alien, with no visa.
9. Causing a public disturbance.
I'll bet They threw The book at
him. He's probably been hoof printed
and is awaiting Trial.

There are some days when I
almost Love This Job.

2/24/10
Here I am at The airport
again. In the atrium, a band
is getting ready to play. And
I have a headache. I know
This isn't talking about driving
Trucks, but it's Something to
write about while I try to
remember Some Truck driving
memories. I Just remembered
Something That happened. It was
in The early 90's. I was on
a run That went up to northwest
Georgia. The messenger was The
Same one That got killed by

33

his wife. I'm going to call
him Cleb. We were finished
with the stops and were about
to go back to Atlanta. Cleb told
me to stop at this burger joint
that was close to the interstate.
Cleb was talking all day about,
having to use the restroom. So
he got out of the truck and
went inside the burger place.
About a half hour to forty-five
minutes later, ol Cleb came
back out smiling. He says
"man, I just blew that place up.
and I've been banned from going
in there anymore." I said, "you
got to be kidding". So I got
out of the truck, and went

inside. When I went in,
The odor was heavy. And Then
there was The restroom itself.
I Should have Stayed out of
the restroom, but I couldn't
because I really had To pee.
So I took a deep breath, and
went in. Right away my eyes
started to get blurry, and burn
Like They do when smoke gets
in them. I was in a hurry To
get done with The Toilet and
get out before I ran out of
breath. On The way back out
to The Truck, Just walking
became a challenge. Every Thing
was blurry and wavy. The
guard riding Shotgun was

Laughing so hard he was
crying. It took more than
one try to get in, or IC the
Truck. Because it looked
like the Truck was moving,
and wouldn't hold still. I finally
got in The Truck, and after
a few minutes we went back
to base.

Winter 2010. Feb.
It was the end of The day.
And this guy, (I'll call him Gomer)
was going to park a company
van for the night. There were
plenty of places to park, but
Gomer passed up a dozen of
Them to squeeze in in someplace

else, I guess Gomer is
as smart as a Lugnut.

March 2010.
I've been working on this book
now, since June of Last year.
And I'm far from finished.
I don't think I've talked about
how I got the nickname
Shotgun. Let's go back to the
year 1988. I got up at about
four o'clock in the morning, and
drive to work. As soon as I
came into the building, the
branch manager would call out
to me "Hey Shotgun! Guard the
front door!" So I would clock
in, and he would give me an

empty Shotgun to guard the
door. He was more Southern
fried than chicken. He would
walk around smoking a cigarette,
and ask people "whatcha doin'
ridin' the clock?". It's hard
to look busy, when you're not.
So I used to smoke cigarettes
with him hoping he wouldn't think
I was riding the clock. He's
not working here anymore. The
last I heard, he was still
having heart attacks. But in
those early days of my driving
armored trucks, we were told
to pull our gun(s) out at every
stop and shoot any son of a bitch,
that held us up. We even had

Shotguns in the trucks with ammo boxes. now some bunch of politically correct pussies ~~that~~ run everything. They don't have a damned clue about what the hell they're doing! I need a cigarette, and my hand is cramping.

4/6/10
I'm at the airport, after driving a regular run. There's a lot of people here for a tuesday. A lot of veterans are here with a lot of gonna be vets. So, I'd like to say Thank you to all of the veterans, active + retired.

The radios in the trucks, back
in the Late 80's + 90's were
really sorry. On the north
Georgia run, the radio would
be useless before we got
to the first stop. Which I
didn't really mind, because I
didn't want to be bothered by
dispatch anyway. The radios
are better now, and I have
mixed feelings about it.
In the early nineties. I drove
a run on occasion that went to
the airport. Those were some
fun days. The run had some
stops around where the planes
came in and went out. So I
would ask the messenger if

we could drag race with The
airplanes. He always said no,
so we never did. One day on
This run, The messenger wanted
to stop at mcDonalds. So we
stopped, and he asked me how
hungry I was. He went in and
got his food, and when I got
back with mine, it got interesting.
It was mid morning and They
were Switching from breakfast
to Lunch. So I got something
Like a bacon, egg, + cheese biscuit,
hash browns, and a quarter pounder
with cheese and a drink. He
asked me, how many apple pies
I could eat. I said I didn't
know. well I wound up in a

ten dollar bet, I had to
eat everything I started
with, _and_ seven apple pies
from mc Donalds before we
got to the next stop. I
don't know how I did it but
I won the bet. Rarely, have
I ever felt so sick. IT
was about six months, before
I could go into another mc Donalds
for anything. That was one
bet I have never repeated.

4/16/10 I have been writing
this book since June of last
year. And I'm not halfway through
it yet. I hope I can come up
with enough to finish it.

Today is the day after
the dreaded April 15 deadline
for tax returns. I'm here at
the Atlanta airport, waiting to
guard for a co-worker. Somebody
is playing the piano, and he
has blue everything on. Blue
coat, pants, & shoes. He plays
good, but keeps playing the
same songs over and over and over.
Enough already! I wish he'd
play something else. I'm starting
to hate that piano. I need to
get away from hearing it, but
there isn't any other place to
sit and write. There's a lot
of people here today and the
noise level makes it hard to

write. I just about miss
driving that run 23, to northwest
Georgia a long time ago. I can't
look at the number 23 without
thinking of that run. The best
apple cider on the planet, comes
from ElliJay Georgia. It was in
one of those small towns, that
I saw a car come down the
road with a bear tied to its
hood. I guess the bear was
the guest of honor at supper,
that night. Driving through the
blue ridge mountains, in a regular
car is one thing. But driving in
these same mountains with an
armored truck is a different
story. Especially when you

have a heavy Load in The Truck.
It gets really hairy if you
don't know The roads that well.
You can really scare The hell
out of The messenger, if you're
Careful about it. I drove a
Truck, on a run to northeast
Georgia, and That Truck was not
good at going up a mountain, at all.
I could LighT a Cigarette, at
The bottom of a mountain, and
be on The second Cigarette, before
we got to The Top of it.
That was a really SLow Truck.

4/27/10   well, it's another
day at The airport. I've got
a Long way to go before I

45

finish this book.
Some where in The 90's,
I was driving The north
Georgia run, and we were
going up a mountain. I was
in The Left Lane, and there
was a car next to me in
The right Lane. The Lady in
The car next to me had
to be Stupid. Because her
Lane was running out, and mine
wasn't. I Looked over at
her, and she had her Son in
her Lap; reading him a book!
I Slowed down, she got
in front of me, and we each
went our own ways. I don't
know where she went, but

I have no doubt, she's still stupid.

4/28/10 I'm at the airport again, and the piano man is still playing the same stale songs. And I'm trying to quit smoking while I sit here, writing this with two packs of cigarettes in my pockets. About ten years ago, I was driving a run, and somebody came up to the truck. He wanted to know if he could make a cash deposit. I told him "yeah," but he changed his mind, and walked away. That piano guy is starting to get on my nerves.

It's The Same Songs everyday.
And it isn't Just The Same
Songs, he keeps playing The
Same Line over & over again.
It's really annoying. Like the
writing is getting Smaller and
Smaller. And it's getting more
difficult To write This Small.
you know what I mean?
I need a cigarette.

5/21/10 Here I am at
The airport again. It's really
busy here, with not enough
seats To go around. The piano
guy is playing again, So I
Think I'll write about an average
day from The merry old days of

yore. I'm in bed, dreaming about palm trees and coconuts. All of a sudden the clock radio goes off. Heavy metal music shatters my dreams, as I shoot *verticaLy straight up out of bed. AC/DC is playing as I struggle to find the switch to turn it off. I turn on the Lamp by the bed, and kill the radio. It's four o'clock in the morning as I sit up and find out there's not a coconut in sight. I can't get my eyes to focus yet, so when I smash my toes on the Leg of the bed, it's followed by a muffled Shhiiiiiitt!

I can't yell, because I'd
wake everybody up, So I
Just Limp into The bathroom
and Try to not Smash anymore
Toes. It's 1989 and I'm still
Living with my family. After I
get done in The bathroom, it's
Time to get dressed. Trying to
Line up my arms and Legs with
The Shirt and pants is a real
Challenge. Finally, I get outside
where my car is waiting, It's
a big bLue '64 Chevy Impala.
The car plays with me, as I
Try to Start it, It Starts
with a menacing growL and
Shudders with The cold air
of The morning, So far it's a

good day, BUT I STarT
shivering with The car on The
way To work. I'm dodging
bums and poTholes as I geT
inTo downTown aTlanTa. when
I get To work, I geT my
STuff Together and go inside.
I'm greeTed with "Hey shoTgun!
guard The front door!" So I
go clock in, and someone hands
me a shoTgun. In The garage,
where The Trucks are loaded,
other people greeT each oTher
with "mornin damniT!" oThers
go with a "oh shiT" To no one
in general. I'll wind up going
out on run 6, with somebody
That looks like "Bubba."

So I spend some time guarding trucks into and out of the building. Then, all too soon, it's time to bring the truck in and get it loaded for the run. My foot doesn't really hurt anymore, it settled into a dull throb a while ago. With the truck inside, I find out it has a lot of boxed coin going out today. I don't know it yet but a surprise is coming my way. I'm loading the quarters, when a box of them falls off the skid, and on my throbbing foot! After the mind blowing pain wears off, we finally get on the run.

The run goes out to the
west side of Atlanta. Our
truck is a god awful looking
thing, that looks retarded.
It's nicknamed a bread truck,
because it looks like one.
This thing is hell on wheels.
It's loud, cramped, cold, and slow.
Anyway, we're going out I20
west, and I can hear the
messenger saying something. It's
a cold morning, and I think he
wants to stop and get something
to eat. So I start yelling
above the engine, McDonalds,!
Burger King!, wendy's!, and he's
still yelling what I think is
eat. So I keep yelling, chick filet!,

quick trip!, Dunkin donuts!,
krispy kreme!, and other places
to eat. well, we get off the
interstate, and we're sitting at
the red light at the end of
the exit ramp. He says "Hey!
you can't hear a goddamned thing
I'm saying, can you." I said "Hell
no. It's noisy up here." He said
"I've been yelling for the heat!
It's cold back here." So I turned
on the heat, and we had a
good laugh about it. the rest
of the day is a blur of things
that happen on the road. Stops
that aren't ready, Burger king
hiring whoppers for .99 cents,
people cutting me off, rain, etc.

After going to about 55
stops, it's time to go back to
base. Getting back into base
is a different story. We drive
up to the door and wait. And
wait, wait, wait. Finally we get
in and park the truck. I have
to finish the route log and
the trip ticket. The route log
shows where we went, what
time we got there + left,
beginning + ending mileage, and
times, etc. The trip ticket shows
that everything was fine before
and after the run. Any problems
with the truck are noted on
the trip ticket. After a while,
the truck is empty and I take

it outside to put fuel in it
for the next day. Fuelling it
takes as long or longer than
getting it into base. About an
hour and a half later, it's fueled
and I have to park it for
the night. By now it's getting
late, but I still can't go home
until the messenger checks the
money into the vault. After he
checks the money in, the
supervisor comes to me, and
says I've been drafted for a
football run. This is not good
news for me, because I've
already been on the clock for
about thirteen to fourteen hours.
But I go on this run too,

because if I don't go, then
they'll fire me. So we get
into a different truck, later
and go on the football run.
The football run only has 3
stops on it, but they expect
us to be at all 3 at the
same time. Needless to say
we only get one stop and
the other 2 stops shut down
before we can get to them.
So we get back to base,
about 2:00 the next morning.
I don't remember driving back
home, but I get there. After
some chicken soup, and about
2 hours sleep, it's time to
get up, and do it again, and

again, and again. For months
at a time, This is how my
days go. Most of the time
I'm working 6 to 7 days a
week with Little or no Time
off. I Still have no idea
how I made it Through
Those days.

6/3/10 Today is a good
day. Yeah, I'm back aT The
airport again. But more
importantly, I'm also halfway
Through This book! It gets
better. The Piano guy isn't
playing The piano!! This is
Great! The day after
tomorrow my vacation Starts.

6/18/10 This year my,
Summer Vacation isn't worth
writing about. So heres
another armored truck,
memory. It was around
1990, or 1991 I was driving
run 23 to northwest Georgia.
We got about half way through
The run, when we had to go
Through a weigh station on
I 75 north. It was summer,
and about a hundred degrees
in The Shade. So we go into
The weigh station to cross over
The scale, and on The way out,
There's an officer standing on
The Side stopping all of The
Trucks. Anyway, he motioned

for me to stop, and I did.
He came over to the truck,
and the messenger in back
asked me why we were
stopping. I had no idea why.
So I told the messenger the
officer wanted us to stop
The officer was a state trooper
with some serious sunburn.
I opened the gun port, and he
asked me if we had any money
on board. I couldn't believe
he was asking such a stupid
question so I told the messenger
about it and he started
Laughing. I told the officer,
we had a little bit of money.
I wanted to tell him,

"no, I'm haulin a bunch of chickens!" but instead, I didn't. I just drove back onto I 75 and kept going.

6/25/10 I've noticed lately that more and more of my writing this book is being done at the airport. Speaking of which, the piano guy is still playing the same songs.
It's busy today, lots of people catching planes, looking for baggage claim, running for the restroom, and wondering where the hell their ride back home is.

7/2/10 Here I am at the airport. The piano guy is still playing, and the day after tomorrow is the 4th of July. The next two days will find me driving runs to Columbus Georgia. And then I'm on vacation for a week. I hope this next vacation goes better than the last one did.

7/12/10 It's monday again, and I'm on the columbus run. My vacation last week, sucked. I spent all week, watching the trees grow, and barking at the dogs. They had it coming to them. The way they looked at me over their shoulder, while they walked sideways past me, spoke volumes. I guess they thought I was crazier than they are. So another vacation has been wasted. But I still have two more weeks to go this year. I'm somewhere in south Georgia, and I think it's going to rain. One more thing about the dogs, they really pissed me off. Barking at everything, and not acting right. I'm on this run again for three more days this week.

7/16/10 I'm still on The
South Georgia run. ~~im~~ And iT
Looks Like I'll be on This
run until sometime in october.
I don't understand people, and
probably never will. There's an
ATM Stop, we go To and I
have To block The driveway To
iT, So iT can be serviced.
And people Still want me To
move The truck. When an ATM
is being Serviced, you can't use
iT anyway. So Some people
Try To back up to iT on The
other Side, and are surprised +
Sometimes angered when They
find ouT They can't use iT.
It's really funny To see Them

Throw a fit. Some of them
start waving their arms, and
cussing, while others look at
me like it's my fault that
they're the ones that are stupid.
It's amazing. we can do so
much with science and technology,
but there just ain't a cure,
or a fix, for stupid.

7/23/10 I'm on a different
run today. It's called the
clean out run. But I just
remembered something I saw
at the airport. There was
a nice looking girl walking
around, and she was wearing
polka dotted rain boots.

It's a beautiful day Today,
The sun is shining, not very
many clouds out, and The
birds are starting To fly a
little funny from The heat.
In other words, It's a day
with a normal amount of abnormal
in it. I'm in a new Truck
too. Somebody else is driving iT
because I don't have a cdL
to drive iT. It's a nice Truck
to ride in because everyThing
still works.

I'm back at The airport
again, and I'm dropping The
idea of writing down The
date.

I still remember the 1996
olympics. Billy Payne Lied
about The summer temps., in
Georgia. The whole thing was
Like a 3 week traffic Jam.
Base was open 24/7.
water, and Lemonade cost about
Three dollars a cup. People
rented out Their houses for
a Thousand dollars a day,
and parking your car in down
Town could cost almost a
hundred dollars a day. And Then
There were the vendors.
Any Thing you could want was.
There with a heavily inflated
price on it.

I Just Saw Somebody walking
Through The airport, with a
chainSaw.

During The olympics, I wound
up on a midnight run to The
federal reserve. IT was
great. At about one Thirty
in The morning, we had break
fast in The Cafeteria. This
was on The Same Scale as
The RiTz. We had real Silver,
Silverware, real Crystal glasses,
China plates, and first class
food. I don't know how, but
The Traffic kept moving. I
Just about ate myself sick
at The federal reserve, but

I really enjoyed that breakfast.
We ate all kinds of stuff,
Bacon, eggs, (fried and scrambled)
Sausage, toast, orange juice, milk,
coffee, hashbrowns, and then
There was the biscuits + gravy,
croissants with jelly, and steak.
And a while after I ate, it
was followed by a good case
of gas. What a day that was!
nobody could get within ten feet
of me after that. I need to
take a break here, because
talking about that breakfast,
has made me hungry.

I still remember seeing
The torch coming down
memorial drive. And what a
crowd There was! People
Lined up all along The streets
and roads for as far as you
could see. When iT got into
down Town Decatur, The messenger
would ask "which way is The
torch going?". And if I said
iT was going to The right, he'd
Say "Go To The Left." I told
anybody That would Listen,
That anytime a torch comes
To ATLanta, Some damn nut
blows up The City. Sure enough,
some damn nut did Try to blow
up The City, JusT Like Sherman

in 1864. I doubt the
olympics will ever come
back to Atlanta.

I probably ought to talk
about my old chevy. It's a
1964 Impala, two door hard
top, that steers like a tank.
It had a 327 V8 when I first
got it. But I blew it up
one morning by accident. Now it
has a 350 V8. This car has
had work done on it from
bumper to bumper. And still it
needs more work. It's taken
me to and from work for a
lot of years. I still remember
starting that car every morning.

IT took Two pumps on The gas pedaL, and Then Turn The key. This car has manual everyThing. Steering, brakes, windows, and seans. I still have The car. But it isn't running at The moment.

Next week I'm going To Columbus, Then the clean out run on Tuesday, and Three other runs.

I remember one morning in The Late 80's, IT was cold and dark. There was rain coming down and, The run started in the bad side of

Town. The car ahead of
me came to a stop, and
There wasn't a stop sign or
stop light. I was wondering
why it was stopping in front
of me. Then I found out
why. The car stopped with
me coming up on it, to let a
damned Squirrel cross the road!
The person driving that car
had to be stupid.

About 20 years ago, I was
just getting started driving
run 6. I'd just made a
left turn from the driveway
at base, when the front end
of the truck started

moving from side to side.
I didn't think much of it
at first, but the more I
drove it, the more it shook.
We were going toward downtown
Atlanta and traffic was
heavy. It was also cold and
rainy. The truck started
shaking a lot worse, and then
it just stopped. But the
engine was still running. The
messenger asked me, why we
stopped. I said, I don't know,
it could be anything. So the
messenger got out to take a
look. When he got back in
the truck, he said "Oh shit."
I asked him what happened.

He said The whole wheeL
on The front of The Truck
had fallen off, and The front
axle was Sitting on The Tire.
Calling This in To dispatch
was a LoT of fun.
me: Hey base!
dispatch: yeah, go ahead.
me: Send me another Truck.
dispatch: why? what's The matter?
me: my Trucks right front wheel
     Just fell off, we're in The
middle of marrietta STreet.
dispatch: <u>Please</u> Tell me
     you're kidding!
me: nope, IT really did happen.
dispatch: aaah Shit! ok Let
me tell The mechanic.

So The mechanics Show up
with another TRUCK, and The
first Thing They Said was
"oh Shit!" I Said, "yeah That's
what I said". After we
Switched TruckS, we were back
on The run again.
Yeah, That was a fun day.

Here's another run 23 flash
back. We were Just Starting
on The run, going up I 75 north,
and about halfway To The first
stop The right rear inside Tire
blew out. BOOM!!!...
I was caught by Surprise,
To Say The Least.

The Truck had a LOT of coin on it, and I damn near changed Lanes without meaning to. So we went Limping up The interstate to The Stop and tried to Lighten The Load. Then The messenger called The tire man To come and fix The tire. We got The tire replaced, and did The rest of The Stops. But on The way back to Atlanta, (yeah on I-75 again going South.) The _Same tire_ blew out again, but more Slowly This time. By This Time we decided To hell with it, and went back to base.

There are three people I'll mention, because I'm bored. I'll just call them, ~~Cleb~~, ~~Clem~~, + ~~Stupid~~ Dumb Ass. These aren't their real names, but I think they graduated from the university of constipation, with "It came Loudly" honors.

It's another lovely day at the airport. Today is payday Friday. I finally got the piano thing licked. I brought my MP4 player. So I don't have to listen to the piano anymore. I bet the piano player has no idea that the song "Dead Skunk in the middle of the road" sounds better than his piano playing.

I saw a sticker on a
car yesterday that said
"Support Zombies". It's nice
to know that some people think
of me.

I was on standby this
morning, and now I'm on sit by
until I go to the airport
at 2:00 this afternoon.
I saw a tag on a car that said
I B OTAY. And I'm not
making it up.
Instead of going to the
airport, I wound up on a
special, that had three stops

on it. This past weekend
was Labor day weekend.
IT was ok I guess, but
who The hell am I kidding?
IT was too short!

Cleb is in The back doing
paper work, so I'll keep on
writing. I wish I had a
dollar for every time, somebody
farted in The truck. It's
The silent ones you have to
Look out for. I remember,
a run we were on in The
mountains. we were way up
on a ridge where you could
see everything. And then
Somebody let one fly.

Yeah, it was one of those silent but deadly farts. I never had a clue about it coming! All of a sudden, the blue ridge mountains were a wide variety of colors. The road, seemed to move like a snake under the truck, and I couldn't get fresh air fast enough! An otherwise normal day suddenly became a _long_ one. Ok, enough of the truck farts. Yesterday I went to the airport again, (yeah, what a surprise!) and caught hell trying to get into a parking lot and park my car.

The LOTS were all "Full"
which means I rode around
The airport at Least _7_ Times
Trying To get a spot. I
finally got in to park because
I guess The parking attendants
felt sorry for me. Oh yeah,
another Lovely day at The
airport. IT wasn't That bad
Though, iT could've been raining.
A Long Time ago, (abouT 5 years)
I invented a new game That
can be played on The road, if
you're going Long distance. IT'S
called "Road kill" after The
dead critters on The side
of The road.

Road kill

Here's how it works.
when you see a dead animal,
on The roadside bring it To
everybody's attention. After
That you have To identify it
to get points for iT.
Don't pull over To Look at it,
because The Skunks really
stink! Here's how The scoring
works.

PTS = Points

Squirrels, crows, etc. — 25 pTs.
~~Dogs~~, cats, possum, raccoons, rabbits, etc.
are 50 Pts.
Dogs, (Large ones.) and other animals
of about The same size, 75 Pts.
Deer, bears, wild hogs, and others
That ~~~~voke a "Holy shit," 100 Pts.
E

When the sun has gone down,
the points double if you can
I.D. the critters.
Bonus points are given for less
frequently seen animals, like
Turtles and snakes. If you
have any questions about this
game, just make it up as
you go along. The one with the
strongest stomach wins.

There's some other people that
I'll mention, but not their real
names. Like, Ellie May, Olive oyle,
and Sara Lou. They are really
nice to know, and talk with but
it's going to be fun to see if
They can figure out who's who!

There are some Trucks
I'll mention. 720 was a Ford
Truck, That had a Cat V-8 in
it. The Tranny was automatic,
and That Thing could run,
Rumor has it That This Truck
could run close to 90 mph.
I don't know if it could
or not, but it could go.

There was another Truck,
15-C That I used To drive.
This Truck could run, but it
was more Sneaky about it.
You could get on The interstate,
with it and before Long The
crazy Thing, would be getting
close to 75 or 80 mph. It was

almost spooky to drive it.
There are some other trucks,
Like 215, 216, 217, 218, that were
Long body trucks. IT was in
one of These Long body trucks
That we went to northwest
Georgia in (remember run 23?)
That cleb got banned from The
burger place.

The piano guy is about to
play again, so you know where
I am today. I'm starting to
Think about getting something to
eat, but I would have to go
outside to escape The piano.

There's not a lot of pages
left to go, and I'm starting
to run low on memories.

Some women came by where
I'm sitting, (about 4) and
asked if they could borrow the
little table I'm using to write
this book on. So I told them
it was ok to use it. A few
seconds later, they decided
to go sit someplace else.
And I got the little table
back.

There's somebody else that
I used to work with. I think
I'll call him Jim Bob. This guy
had four dads. He had his

bioLogicaL dad, of course,
and Then there were,
dad gummiT, dad burniT, &
dad bLame iT. Now, Jim Bob (as far
as I can Tell.) never used any cuss
words ThaT were STronger Than
"fooT", or one of his other dads
names. BuT one day on a over
The road run, base managed To
piss off ol Jim Bob. I don't remember
The detaiLs, but Some Thing in
Jim Bob Snapped. Because, all of
a sudden This TorrenT of profanity
expLoded out of Jim Bob. I was
really shocked aT firsT, because
iT came out of nowhere. With
no warning he LeT Loose with
everyThing in The book. Maybe,

It was all those years of
not cussing that built up.
He started with dadburnit
and foot. Then came the
damnits, goddamnits, shits,
motherfuckers, and all the rest
of it. Coming from Jim Bob,
it was so funny I couldn't
help laughing. The more he
cussed at base on the radio,
the harder I laughed. After
a while, he started running
low on steam for cussing at
base. I couldn't help laughing
the whole time. I laughed
until I thought hyperventilation
wasn't too far away. I haven't
seen Jim Bob for a long time,
since.

But That day, we both
had a good Laugh.

I'm on The columbus run
again, and it's a nice day.
I should have Left the onions
off The hotdogs I ate Last
night. Yesterday was Sunday,
and I wound up on a run That
was really Long. IT wasn't The
amount of STops That we had,
we Just didn't know where
The hell we were going!
But after about 234 miles,
we got iT finished.
Zeb is in The back, and we
don't have much more to go.

This is a good day. Its
Friday, payday, and The piano
guy isn't playing anyThing.
On top of all This I also
have a three day weekend
coming.

I wish I had a dollar for
every stupid thing I have
seen happen and for all The
bumps I've been over. If I
did, I could retire right now.

I'm not sure, but I think the
piano guy went and got a
mohawk haircut. He did !
I wonder if he knows how he
Looks, because I feel Like

I'm about to barf up the
steamed rice I just ate.
I just fed a dollar to
the crazy chair I'm sitting
in. It's one of those massage
chairs, that eats your money,
and then tries to kill you.
I want to shoot the chair
but I can't, because it's out
of season.

I'm going to call the piano guy,
mohawk. Because he just
got started playing again.

I still remember the
savings + loan failure of the
90's. Everybody was looking

at the truck I was driving,
Like a hungry cat Looks at
a bird. I couldn't help
wondering if I was going
to have to shoot somebody,
or not. But Luck was with
me, and I didn't have to shoot
anybody.

There was somebody else,
I'll mention. His name will
be changed to Zeke. Zeke
had a semi-auto 9mm, holster,
Laser sight, etc. And he could
barely hit the broad side
of creation with it. He had
over a thousand dollars tied
up in this stuff.

Anyway, Zeke quit one
day and became a Lock Smith.

There's another old favorite,
Thing to do in The Trucks.
But you can only do it in
The older Trucks. It's called
"gun port Snapping." Some of
The older Trucks have Spring
Loaded gun ports on The doors.
We would be at a Traffic
Light, and see somebody in
a car with The window, rolled
down, or a Convertible with
the Top down. Then, while
Looking ahead, and without
actually opening it, I'd Snap
The gun port, Just To See

what they would do. We got
some of the funniest looks
from people. Some times the
messenger would rock side to
side, in his seat and get the
truck rocking side to side, while
sitting still at a light. Again,
we got some really strange
looks from people. Those
were some really fun days.

I'm on the columbus run
today and I've already seen
a bunch of road kills. I even
saw a deer eating close to
the edge of the woods. But
I can't count the deer, because
it was still alive. And the

game is Road kill. So Living critters don't count.

While I try to think of more memories to write about, I'll just wing it for now. I'd like to thank all the people (Living and dead), that helped make the memories that are in this book. Also, all the people who are buying my book, Thank you very much. And I want to thank my friends and family for being there, any time I needed them. Thank you.

I just remembered, a long time ago, I used to ask new people, if they checked the turn indicator fluid in the truck. There isn't any such thing, but some of them tried to find and check it anyway. It was always good, for a laugh.

It's october again, and there's a lot of veterans at the airport. Hold up season is here, and when I'm driving a run, I stand a chance of getting shot or blown up at any given stop.

There's a stack of news papers right next to me and they're (I think) written in Chinese. Anyway, I have a feeling ole mohawk is about to start playing the piano again.

The pages are starting to run out, so I'll mention somebody else. I'll just call him clem. He drives the bigger trucks, like the fed truck and the clean out run. Both of those trucks have a short run, in the number of stops that they have.

Clem used to be in the marines. He's been driving armored trucks for 25 years. Clem and I used to talk about different ways to catch airplanes. We came up with some crazy ideas, but never tried them.

Anytime the truck breaks down, the truck that we switch over to backs up, and we switch trucks, back to back.

This month is one for the book. It's october, and some strange things are happening.

Earlier This month, one of my co-workers died from natural causes. He was old.
Another one, (who I'll call Dumbass) got locked up for stealing money. And a few days ago, somebody else, blew his nose with a gun. Services for him will be This weekend.
Anyway, here we sit in South Georgia, taking a break.
It looks Like it's going to rain.

I think I've officially run out of memories (unless I can think of more.) to talk about.

So I guess I'll put The end
of The book stuff here.

I want To Thank everybody,
friends, family, Co workers, and
The people who gave me The
memories To write This book.
Even Though I can't remember
all Their names.

The people That I did write
about, will have To Try To figure
out who's who, because I forgot,
who's who.
There's one more person I
want To mention. His name will
be Changed To SLim. He's been
a good friend, but he's dying,

from cancer. A LOT of people
will miss him.

Well, I guess this is it.
The last page, of the book.
It's a good thing, because
I just ran out of stuff
to write about. OL mohawk
just got cranked up on the
piano.
He's still playing the same
thing. Writing this has been
an experience. And now the space
on the page is running out. So I
have to write smaller and smaller,
to get all of this stuff in.
That piano is getting on my nerves.
I need a cigarette. Have a good day.

HILLBILLY ARMORED, INC.

HILLBILLY ARMORED, INC.

PART II

WELCOME TO
BETWEEN GROCERY

00002545150   BETWEEN GROCERY
1991 HWY 78   BETWEEN GA

Descr.	qty	amount
T HIGH TAX GROCERY	1	1.79
T HIGH TAX GROCERY	1	0.99

Sub Total		2.78
Tax		0.19
TOTAL		**2.97**
CASH $		5.00
Change $		-2.03

THANKS, COME AGAIN

REG# 0001 CSH# 002 DR# 01 TRAN# 16411
08/11/10 13:48:55   ST#   1

HillBilly Armored Inc. Part 2

Hey! welcome back, To HillBilly Armored Inc. And another heaping helping of more fun stuff, to read about. Let's see,... 2011 is off to a roaring start. In January, cleb (This is a different cleb.) got shot at an atm about 9 times. The bad guy's came around the blind side of the truck, and got him. Cleb, is still alive and, doing as well as can be expected. Nobody knows when, or if cleb will be coming back to work.

Today, is Friday and I drove a regular run, but I also

wound up going out to the
airport. Yeah, it came as no
surprise to me though.
There's a Jazz band playing,
and it's so loud, that there's
no way you can hear yourself
Think. I Just hope my mp3
player keeps playing for me.
It's 5:33 in the evening
and I can't wait to get out
of the airport. Anyway, enough
of the sorry Jazz band.
My first week of vacation
isn't too far away, so I'm
looking forward to that.

So here we go again, at
the airport. There's a woman

Sitting two seats from me
and she's wearing fuzzy
slippers. I just got through
driving a run in and around
Buckhead, and now I'm sitting
in the airport writing this
book. Yesterday on the
clean out run, we got hammered
by a violent rain storm. It
rained so hard, that visibility
was almost zero. Today, on
the other hand has been great
with the weather. But the
people out there are something
else altogether. There's a lot
of gonna be vets here today.

The Last time I was at the airport, The average crowd was here. Tomorrow, I'm on The columbus run again. I have been Lucky enough to get Some Georgia moonshine Jelly, at a place between columbus and La grange Georgia.

Well, Today is a nice day for being on a run! The Sun is cut, and it's great. we're Taking a break, right now and Then we'll finish The run. People still cut me off all The time, and it's really annoying! And They're always on The Telephone!

I don't know what I'll do
on vacation next week, but
I'm sure going to find out.

I just saw a red pick up
truck go by, with a plate on
the front that said "moose".
It's funny what some people
name their vehicles. I don't
think the person in the red
pick up, knows what a moose
looks like.

I'm going to back up to
9/11/01 now. That day started
like any other day. It was
clear, sun shining, and just
beautiful. I was driving

a run that went up and down Buford highway. I think the run was old run 5. Anyway, about midmorning the messenger came out of a stop, and told me that the World Trade center in new york city had just been hit by an airplane. At first, I was in disbelief, and a mild state of shock. Later that day, I saw the footage on TV and there aren't enough words to describe how I felt. And here we are, in 2011. I get a feeling the terrorists, will try something again this year.

Yesterday somebody at a
different armored carrier, got
shot and killed at a stop.
I don't have any other details,
about it.

A long time ago, I was
driving an over the road run, with
Cleb. It went way out to the
other side of nowhere. But we
had to find a new stop, and
off we went. So after a few
miles, we came to this little
town with a square in the
middle of it. And just off
the square was a police car
That was watching us. We

Started going around The Square
Looking for The road That we
needed To turn onTo but
couldn't find right away. About
3 Laps around The Square LaTer,
we STill didn't See iT. By This
time The officer was Looking
at us with a LoT of interest,
and probably wondering what
The hell was going on! Another
five Laps LaTer we were
STarting To get dizzy, So we
STopped and asked The officer
for directions. He Said he was
wondering how many more Times
we were going To go around
The Square, and we Told him
abcut one more Time ought To

do iT. Finally we found The
Stop, and on our way back To
The interstate, we did one more
Lap around The Square. And then
we went back To base.
You can't buy fun Like That
with money!

Yesterday, I drove a regular
run, and about Six or Seven
Stops into iT, The Truck died.
So we wound up about Two and
a half hours behind Schedule.
we finished The run aT about
5:30, which isn't too bad.
writing This is getting difficult,
because I've got a case of gas!
I'm going To Take a break now

because my eyes hurt.

I haven't been to the airport for a while, so I'm writing at the dentist's office today. I actually like coming here, because it's pain free. But I still hate getting my taxes done.

I remember a long time ago, coming back from a run and getting into downtown Atlanta. Everything was jammed up with traffic. It turns out the Grateful dead were in town for a concert.

I never had so much fun
being stuck in Traffic!
There was all kinds of stuff
to see. Like barefoot girls
with flowers in Their hair, and
not wearing any bras. Also,
VW vans from The sixties with
peace signs all over Them, and
plenty of flowers. I havent
seen so many hippies in one
place since The sixties. They
were everywhere. Tall, short,
hairy, and braless people as far
as you could see. And Tents
popped up, in every parking lot,
public park, and any place you
could set up camp. A lot of
people were smoking, but I

wonder how many of the ciggy's were legal. It must have been alright, because everybody was happy. Even the messenger liked what he saw going on. I still wonder when the Grateful dead will come back to Atlanta, so I can see more hippies getting drunk and having a good time with flower power, vans, tents, and everything Sixties.

I haven't been on the airport run in a while, but it's ok because the clean cut run is also a good run to be on.

Tomorrow I'm scheduled to
be on a regular run, and
Friday also. But I have this
weekend off. well, it rained
all weekend and I'm into another
week. Today I'm on a good run,
and it's only Tuesday.
We're at a money center, and
everybody is waiting for shipments.
The talk is about sports, among
other things. So, I'll keep on
writing this book. I'm probably
going to be on three more
different runs before the week
is over. It's ok though because
it just means "more cheese
on the pizza". I like a good
cheesy pizza.

OK, here's some stuff about
armored trucks, you might not
know about.

1. Staying warm in winter,
   wear Long Johns, and hope the
   heat in the truck works. This
   applies to the old vintage trucks.

2. Gun control. Don't miss the
   target.

3. Eating + soft drinks.
   Don't eat anything that you'll
   wind up wearing, And always
   get a drink with a resealable
   cap.

There's some other stuff, but I'll get to that later.

Years ago, I saw somebody in downtown Atlanta, that was preaching to a <u>tree</u>. With a bible, and at the top of his lungs. There was nobody else around him.

I'm on the cleanout run today, and it's another good day.
The cleanout run went great yesterday, and now I'm on the airport run today. There's somebody else I'll talk about, and I'll call him Cletus.

Cletus is the head mechanic at the shop. He's a real good person, and a good friend. The other mechanics are also good friends.

I'm sitting in the airport atrium now, and Mohawk is standing there staring at the piano!

I'm on the Columbus run today, and Zeb is in the back. There's a union meeting this evening, so I have to get back to base in time to make it.

Hillbilly armored Just recently bought another armored company, So That means Hillbilly armored inc., Just got bigger!
Nobody knows what to Think about it. I know what I Think about it, and I don't give a damn about it.

IT's another day at The airport, and I hope mohawk Called off Sick. Tomorrow is The dreaded Apr. 15th! Besides That, mohawk Just got cranked up on The piano. Some Lady Just walked by wearing SomeThing That makes her look Like a multi-Colored potatoe chip. The walking Tater chip, just came around for the third time. She'll probably (yeah, she dJust did Lap number 4) come around for number 5. She just did Lap 5, and I wonder how many more She'll do. Yep, I'm at the airport. Tater chip is still doing Laps around the atrium. This is a really fun day. Tomorrow I'm on a regular run again, and it'll probably be a 15 to 16 hour day. Ol' Tater Just did Lap 9 or 10, but I'm not counting anymore.

On 4/17/11, my good friend and
former co-worker Slim died
from cancer. Today is the
21ST and I still can't believe
he's ~~dead~~ dead. His friends
and family are feeling a great
Loss. I will never forget
The example and ideas That
Slim showed me for Living
Life in general.

OK, it's time to get back.
To Truck memories. I have
driven Trucks with bugs in
Them, And a Lot of Those
Trucks had anTs in Them.
There were days when I
Spent half my time driving

The Truck, and The other
half killing ants. And on
more Than one occasion, I've
had bees fall into my Lap,
because They came in Through
The air vent above me. And
of course, it always happened
on The interstate. The bees
always would Look around Like
They were wondering what
The hell was going on. But I
Still managed to kill Them To.

There's a bad Storm coming
Later today, and I hope iT
holds off until I'm back home.
over The years, I've had
Some imaginary guards with

me in The Truck. So far The
LiST includes names Like The
following. Rigor morTiS, Seymour
ButTS, ~~I.~~ P. Daily, I. P. Freely,
I. M. Gassy, Sir osiS of Liver,
Sir Pee aLoT, CLaude Balls, eTC.
Any SimiLariTy beTween The
names above, and Living people
(~~wheTher~~ weTher reaL or imagined.)
is a crying Shame!

I have JusT recenTly found
ouT ThaT hillbilly armored inc.
has boughT anoTher armored Truck
company. This doesn't make
any sense, because hillbilly armored
inc., is claiming ThaT They ain't
making any money!

And if they ain't making any money, how the hell can they buy up the competition! Yeah, it's a real head scratcher alright.

We're taking a break now, and Zeb is doing paperwork. That storm is getting close, and it might get us on the way back to base. We still need to fuel the truck to.

This Friday, I'm going to be back at the airport again, trying to think of more stuff to write in this book.

So far This year, I've already
had one "Stay cation" and iT sucks
because The price of gas, is
almost at 4.00 a gallon. I hope
my vacations are better This
year, Than They were Last year.

Today is Friday, and I'm back
at The airport. Mohawk isn't
playing The piano anymore, but
instead he's playing an
electric keyboard. The crowd
is Thin today, but That's ok.
I wonder if ol Tater found
her flight.

There's somebody else I used
to ride on The run with

a Long Time ago. I'll Just call him Big Bubba. Now Bubba, was really big. I remember he needed not one, but Two gun belts hooked Together, to get around his waist. And he used some kind of cheap after shave or Cologne That was probably called dead skunk number nine. IT Stunk so bad I had to fart again and again To make The truck smell better! But in The end The Truck, smelled Like a farting dead Skunk. I hated riding with him on a run.

I don't remember if I've
written about this or not,
but I guess I'll mention it
now. It was run 23 a long
time ago. I was up in north
Georgia, driving down the
road when I noticed that
the oncoming traffic was doing
something strange. They were
going way around my truck
when they passed me. At
first I didn't pay any attention
to it, but after a while
I figured out why. The battery
door on the driver's side of
the truck was open and flapping
in the wind. So I told the
messenger about it, and at the

nexT STop The messenger
Tied iT ShuT with a metal
CoaT hanger.

There was some good news
This week. Osama bin Laden
was killed!!!! I'm really
happy ThaT The Son of a Bitch
is dead. There's a LoT of
veTerans (Guess where I'm at)
here Today. And mohawk hasn't
Started playing yet. I'm going
To go have a Cigarette while
I wait for another memory
To come To me.

I remember coming back from run 23 a long time ago. This semi flat bed truck came by me, and on the flat bed trailor was a <u>Toy</u> Tonka dump Truck strapped down with a chain. Yeah, some things you just never forget.

I have been to (Believe it or don't) between, Georgia. No, I'm not kidding. There really is such a place. And it's between Loganville and manroe Ga. It's not a very big place, but it does have a gas station, with a working toilet.

OK, I looked it up on my
hillbilly gps (a map) and heres
the directions.

Loganville   *Between*   monroe
_____
         Hwy 78

West   East
⟵   ⟶

Anyway, today is wednesday
and tomorrow I'm on the
airport run again. I don't mind
though, because I like it.

I spent a lot of thursdays
on run 23, and that brings
me to another memory.

we were on our way back
to Atlanta, on I-75 South.
I was just driving along, and
everybody else in the truck
was sleeping. After a while,
I was running next to a
semi, and the other truck
driver noticed that the guard
who was riding shotgun was
sound asleep. well, the other
truck driver in the semi must
have been bored, because he
reached up, and blew his
trucks air horn. The sleeping
guard riding shotgun next to
me, just about went through
the roof of the truck! The
semi driver was laughing so

hard, he had to pull over and
get out to pee. The guard
on the other hand, headed for
the restroom when we got back
to base. I just laughed until
I could barely breathe anymore.
The look on the guards face
when the air horn blew, was
priceless. That guard isn't with
us anymore, (ha, ha, ha!) I wonder
why.

Summer is almost here,
and I get the feeling it's
going to take me another
year to finish this book.
I saw a car on the
road today, and the head

Lights had eyelashes on
Them. And they were blowing
in The wind on The interstate.

Well, old mohawk is playing
again, and I don't have any
way to really escape it, unless
I go outside. I'm not quite
at the halfway point with
This book yet, but I'm starting
to get close to it.

I drove a run yesterday,
That will stick out in my
memory for a while. The
messenger went into The stop,
which was a wal-mart and
called me on my radio,

To inform me that he was sitting on the toilet and dropping a shit. I just sat there in the truck, staring at the radio and wondering what he was thinking. I know what I was thinking! And that was, what the hell do I care about what he's doing in the restroom! I'll just call him I. P. Daily.

I'm back at the airport today, and it's an average day. The veterans are coming and going, but some of the people look like zombies. As a matter of fact, some of them act and

even smell like Zombies.
The memories are coming to
me slower and slower, so it's
time for a cigarette, break.

OK, here's a news flash.
Today is Friday 5/20/11, and
rumor has it, that tomorrow
will be the end of the world.
They say it's going to happen
at about 6:00 or 6:30 in the
evening. I guess it would
be a good idea to stock up
on beer and other stuff tonight.
Well, maybe there's not much
sense in doing that anyway.

There was a Truck I drove
a Long Time ago. And The
wiring was crossed up in iT.
IT Started raining, So I
flipped The Switch for The
wipers, and The Siren came on.
So I turned That off, and
Tried again. nexT I Tried The
Siren Switch and The running
Lights came on. By This Time
I was running out of Switches
To Try, So I Tried The running
Lights Switch, and The wipers
Started working.

And Then There was The
Special run I drove one Time.
A Special run Though, only

has one or two stops on it.
we got in the truck and I
noticed the fuel gage was
on empty. So I told the
messenger about it and he
told me not worry about it.
Naturally I asked him why.
He told me the fuel gage
worked backwards, and that
as long as it was on empty
we were ok. And if it
started going to full, then
we would have to stop for
more fuel. Yeah, the fun
never stops.
There was another special
run I drove at night.
But this truck had

Cross eyed headLights.

The memories are coming
back to me but I need
a break.

I have seen a lot of
neat places and Things over
The years, but I can't
remember how to get back to
Them.

But I remember driving
some runs when I'd be driving
down The road, and ask The
messenger about where to Turn
at. I would ask "Do I turn
right at The second Light?",

and for some reason, the
messenger would tell me "no,
turn right at the second light."
Things like that have happened
a lot, and still continue to
happen. I'm having a "staycation"
this week. Yesterday was
6/8/11 and I installed a new
dishwasher in the kitchen.
Believe me, it's not fun, but
my son helped so it wasn't
too bad. Today I'm at the
dentist office again. The
woman working on my mouth
today is MerLou. She's really
nice, and always in a good
mood. As usual, I changed
her name. MerLou is her

name for This book.

I'm back on The cleanout run Today. IT sure is hot out here. The Tempeture is Supposed To be in The 90's Today. And ThaT brings me To anoTher memory. I was driving a run a Long Time ago, about The middle of July. IT was old run 6, and about 10:00 or 10:30 in The morning, The A/C quit. ThaT Truck became a rolling oven on wheels. We couldn't go back To base, because we had So many sTops To go To.

So instead, we took turns
buying rounds of gatorade.
I was running through that
stuff by the quart! And so
was the messenger. All of
the air vents, and the fans
were open and turned on.
We were sweating so much,
that neither of us had to
pee. I drank every flavor
that Gatorade had to offer,
and still put away at least
eight quarts. It was about
105 degrees that day.

Sometimes I like to play
with the new people, that
get hired here.

I'll casually tell Them To
Check The turn indicator fluid
in The Truck. Sometimes They
Lock for iT under The hood,
and once in a while I geT
Cletus To help Them with iT.
You remember Cletus The
head mechanic.

Today is wednesday and I'm
on a run, but Taking a break.
IT's hoT as hell outside, but
The A/C is sTill working.

Here's anoTher run 23
memory. I was driving
somebody, I'll call Clem. I
Think Clem was a Little

hard of hearing, because
going down The road, I
could ^Tell him his ass was on
fire, "and he'd say "That's
nice". But The Truck was
so Loud iT was hard for
him 70 hear what I was
saying anyway. Clem isn't
around anymore because he
died in The first book from
old age.

Some Times I wonder abouT
where The people who LefT
This Job have gone.
I JusT Saw Some girL
Throw up in The parking LoT.

They say it's going to rain
all this week. I hope it
doesn't. Today's imaginary guard
is Rigor Morris. And I.P.
Daily, will be riding with me
for the rest of the week.
Next week we have an imaginary
guard coming from England.
His name is Sir Osis of Liver.
And somebody else, by the
name of Sir Lottagas. They
were in the war of "The baked
beans". I'm going to take a
break, and try to remember
some more stuff.

Ok, I have somemore to talk about. On Tuesday This week, I was driving a run when The fan belt on The engine Jumped off. This isn't SomeThing That you want To happen in any vehicle, Let alone an armored Truck. We parked it in The Shade of a Tree in The parking Lot, and Shut it off. Then I got on The radio and called for help. It Took only minutes for That Truck to get hot as hell inside. A while Later They brought us another Truck, and we were on our way again.

But then The A/c in The
other Truck quit working,
and it was hot in That
Truck for The rest of The day.
We couldn't Switch Trucks
again, because There wasn't any
more Trucks available.
That was a real Long day.

A Long Time ago, I was on
a run in downtown Atlanta,
Sitting at a Stop, And There
Was some nut walking
around Knocking on peoples
car windows. He was bumming
money, and wasn't having any
Luck. Finally he came over
to The Truck I was

driving, and tried his luck
with me! He changed his
mind in a hurry, when he
saw me. ~~gun~~. After a while
a police car showed up, and
There was a lot of talking
and arm waving going on. And
Then another police car showed
up. One of The officers
got on his radio and a
paddy wagon showed up. So
The window knocking nut
got hauled away.

The 4th of July is tomorrow
and Then I'm on The columbus
run, Tuesday Thru Friday
This week.

Each day will start extra
early because they won't
load the coin the night before.
It just means I'll get
enough hours,

I remember when we had
shotguns in all the trucks.
And a ammo can stuffed full
of rounds for everybody in
the truck. People would go
the long way around you
when they saw that scatter
gun in your hands. The idea
back then was to kill the
bad guys.

Back in The good ol' days,
when gas was only (about) a
dollar a gallon, I was on a
run in The middle of nowhere.
This Lady came out of The
building That was our stop.
She was carrying The stuff
That she had just bought, out
To her car. Well, she got her
car key out, unlocked The door
and opened it up. Now I know,
This doesn't sound <u>That</u> unusual,
but The car was a convertible,
and <u>The Top was down,</u> IT
made me wonder, why The
hell she Locked it in The
first place!

And another time, on a different run, we were at a gas station. I was just sitting there waiting, when I saw a car in the parking lot close by with a woman and baby sitting in it. The baby must have been hungry, because the woman reached into her shirt and pulled her boobs out. Yeah, that baby settled down in a hurry! The woman had no idea that she had caught the attention of a very horny truck driver. Some memories do stand the test of time!

I Just checked, and This
page is The half way point
for This book. After This second
half is finished, I Think I'll
be done writing for a long while.
I Think I'll celebrate This
half way Thing, by Staring at
my Spare Change I've been
Saving.

OK, That's enough excitement,
Let's get on with The Last
half, of This book.

It looks Like it might
rain Today, but we don't have
That much more To do out here.

Tomorrow I'm on the fed
run. I haven't been on that
for a long time.

Believe it or not, some
people have asked me if I
have real bullets in my gun!
And sometimes I want to
tell them, "no, it shoots
sweet potatoes instead!".
I wonder what the hell these
people are thinking. One
person thought I was driving
an ice cream truck. And
another thought it was a
pizza truck! come on! no
Ice cream or pizza truck has
gun ports on it.

A long time ago, on the way back to Atlanta, I saw a great big Lobster on a truck bed. This thing was huge! The claws ~~alon~~ alone were the size of a midsize car. And Just in case anybody is wondering, no it wasn't alive. But if Lobsters ever do get that big, you'll need a machine gun to kill them.

I recently wound up on a run that goes up to the mountains. It's a nice Little run, with a Lot of driving up and down the hillbilly highway.

We're taking a break now,
but a stop for fuel isn't
too far away.

There is somebody else that
doesn't work here anymore, and
I'll just call him dumbass.
I saw a picture of him and
his wife (?) and I could not
tell which one was the wife!
And to make it worse, they
have about three kids. And
ol'e dumbass once told me
that he spent seven years
in high school. He should have
signed up for the life time
plan.

The old bread trucks, were
a real pain to drive. Every
time you turned the steering
wheel, the seat would turn
in the opposite direction.
So when I turned to make
a right, the driver seat would
rotate to the left. Ok, it's
time to forget the dreaded
bread trucks.

There's another route manager
who wants his name changed
to otis. He's a good friend, but
for some reason, he took the
nickname Kung Fu Panda.

August is here, and The
summer is almost over.
Some people think The world
will end on 12/21/12, next
year. I don't know, but I
hope I can finish writing
This book before it gets
here. It'd be Just my
Luck To get This Thing
finished on 12/20/12!

There's another person That
I have known a Long Time.
I'll call her Thelma Jean. She
works upstairs on The computer,
but I still remember when
she used To go out on a run.

And some others come to mind. Barbee Sue, has been here a long time and still drives a run. Bettie Lee has been here a little while, and she's real nice. Barbee Sue says hey!

It's not too hot today, but I think it's going to rain on us before we get back.

And there's another cleb that's been here a real long time. He drives a pickup truck. Zeb is in the back, and we're taking a break.

I better get going because
break time is over.

Today is payday Friday.
Yesterday somebody retired,
so I'll call him Billybob.
O'le Billybob had a habit of
saying "you know?" with every
thing he said. You know?
He was a good person, and
should enjoy retirement.
This week in Augusta,
somebody was attacked at an
ATM. He's still alive, but that's
about all I know.

A long time ago, in a land far, far, away (Sound familiar?) There was a truck stuck on a railroad crossing. The driver was poking at the engine with a screw driver. I didn't think anything of it at the time, but when I came back a while later, the truck was gone. I thought the guy got it fixed and went on his run. About three days later, I found out what really happened. A freight train came along and took the truck with it, eleven miles down the tracks. The entire eighteen wheel semi was gone.

Remember That Truck I Told
you about, a few pages back?
The one where The belT Jumped
off The engine? I was on
a run recently, with ThaT Same
Truck and it broke down
again! But This time the
engine kepT running and Just
The a/c quit working. I
wanted To Shoot The damned
Thing, but iT's against Company
policy To waste bullets
Shooting a Truck.

IT's a different day ~~another~~
and another week. I'm on
a different run every day.
But it's ok because I Like

cheese. There's yet another
person I'll put in the book.
This book is starting to get
a little cramped for all the
people I'm putting in it.
The next one, I'll call
Earnest T. He's as country
as a cornfield, but he's
been working here for about
thirty five years.

I'll be going (I think anyway)
to the airport this Friday,
So you'll probably see me
mention Ole mohawk again. But
his hair is growing back so
the mohawk is almost gone.

Anyway, Today is monday
and I'm down in (almost),
SouTh Georgia again. Check
The hillbilly GPS below.

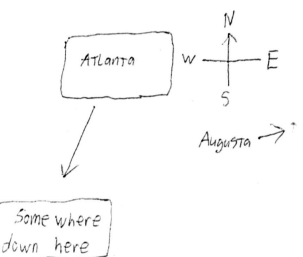

This map (hill billy GPS) is not
drawn To Scale, So don't Try
To use iT.

Thursday This week, I'll
be up in the mountains on
The hillbilly highway again.
Don't make me go GPS on
you again, (I might start Liking
it!) but I will if I have to.

The Summer is almost over,
and soon The Traffic will be
heavy again with everybody
going somewhere, or nowhere
for The holidays.

I recently saw Three deer
Standing on The side of the
interstate, eating grass.

Daniel R. Poncinie

A Long Time ago, on old run 23 (you remember) I was driving South on US 27 about ten miles outside of Rome Georgia. There was a Log Truck ahead of me and I noticed the trailer was smoking. As I got closer, I saw one of the trailer tires was on fire. It was also flinging pieces of flaming tire tread everywhere.

So I got up next to the truck with the flaming tire and used the P/A to tell the other truck driver what was going on. One look in his mirror, and he pulled over to

The side of the road to put it out. I can just imagine what the guy's reaction was, as he put out the tire.

This summer, I saw another semi in the middle of I-75 and the whole tractor was on fire. The fuel tanks were also burning, and the heat was so intense, nobody could get close enough to put it out. Also, the front part of the trailer was burnt.

Well, 9/11 came and went
again without incident.
And This week, I'm on at
Least Three different runs.
The weather has cooled
down quite a bit. The
critters will be moving around
more.

Yesterday, was my 23rd year
anniversary for driving armored
TruckS. I'm So happy, I could
Just Shit.

Anyway, There's Talk going
around That Some of The
runs will get Changed To

Some degree. IT basically
means That more people
won't have any idea where
The hell they're going.
But Then, This IS hillbilly
armored inc.

I'm going to Take a minute,
To Talk about The management
in ~~nowhere~~ Those xer a peein,
dickheads need To go Fuck
a pinetree!

Ok, I feel normal again.
By The way, CTIS doesn't
work here anymore, so cleb
(This is a different cleb) Took

his place. well, it's The
STart of another week,
and I'm on a different run
every day.

Remember dumbass from The
first book? You know, The
one who robbed an armored
Truck and got caught? well,
he's facing his Sentenceing
next year on Jan 4. He
admitted To doing it, so he's
going To prison for a Very
Long Time.

Today is wednesday, and I'm
on The columbus run again.
Were Taking a break, and I

really need to pee.
I'm starting to wonder if
and when I'll be on the
airport run again. I hope
it's soon. There's some more
people I want to get in the
book, and here they are.
First, is Hank. Now, Hank
takes care of stuff at base.
He sweeps, mops, etc. He's been
doing that for a good while.
Then there's Sophie Lou. She
works in the vault, and she's
real nice.
I think it's time for me to
take a break from writing, because
my hand is getting tired.

Another memory Just came
To me. Yeah, it's another Run
23 memory. I can't help it;
a LOT of Stuff happened on
That run. IT was a regular
day (as regular days go) and
we had a vintage Truck, with
a little over a ~~hundred~~ hundred boxes
of coin on iT. Along with The
currency, and bagged Loose coin
on The Truck to. The Truck
was so overLoaded, Thon when
we goT on The interstate with
iT, we couldn't keep up with
The Traffic. I remember
calling To The Messenger over
my Shoulder and Saying, "Hey!
we're up To 40 miles an hour!"

I'm on a different run
Today, and I Saw a bush
with a mohawk! IT was
in La Grange Georgia. It's
Like a Summer day Today.
no wonder I'm Seeing Strange
Things. Also, There was a car
Thatt Tried To go around Some
road construction, and got hung
up on The edge of The road.
Because The Shoulder of The
road had been Lowered by
about 18 inches.

Later This week, I'll be back
at The airport again, but I
don't mind iT.

There's somebody else I'll
put in here. She's the woman
I guard at the airport. I'll
change her name to Annie Lynn.

In a roundabout strange kind
of way, I'm looking forward
to going back to the airport
again. I miss the smell of
jet exhaust, people trying to
find a toilet in a hurry, and
can't speak english, and the
ones that wound up at baggage
claim, when they were trying
to catch a connecting flight,
and their baggage took off
without them. Oh, the airport
is so much fun!

There's Somebody who works
upstairs at base. I'll call
her Jo Leen. She works with
route Logs, and a computer.
She's been There for a Long
Time.

Today is payday Friday, and
I'm at The airport again.
It's not That busy Today
but There's still ~~interop~~ interesting
people here.

A Long time ago, I was
driving a run That went up
Buford highway. And I Saw
Somebody driving a white
pick up Truck.

This person was shaving his
head with an electric razor!
Oh well, I've seen crazier
stuff than that, right?

Today is columbus day, and
this week might be alright.

Today I saw somebody
that I'll call redcoat. He was
at a stop that we were at,
and he was nuttier than a
walnut tree. He was talking
to the garbage can, and having
a conversation with it and
the truck I was driving.

This week has turned out
to be a good week at
hillbilly armored. But I found
out that earlier this year,
one of the old branch managers
died in June. He was the one
That gave me the nickname
"Shotgun".

There's a lot of future veterans
here at the airport today.
And it's raining outside.
I Just Saw Somebody walk
by, and it Looked Like they
were wearing pajamas.
You know I'm running Low
on armored truck memories
when I start talking about

people wearing paJamas at
The airport. I'm going out
for another Cigarette, because
The piano is cranked up again.

I Saw a girl walk Through
The airport with really bright
metallic neon pink hair.

I was driving a run in The
early 90's, and as we're
going down The road, This car
comes flying up on my right
side. All of a sudden, it cuts
in front of me and Stops!
I couldn't believe what
was happening. So I checked
my mirror on The right side

and nobody was There, So I was able To go around the car. As I got next To it, I Looked over and, The Two guys in The car were <u>Laughing</u> at what They had Just done. I got So mad, I wanted To empty The Shotgun into Them. But I couldn't do That, because Some how it's against The Law To Shoot a dumbass. Even Today I'm Still amazed at how Stupid Some people are.

well, Halloween is almost here, and The holiday Season Starts. I'm on The South Georgia run again, and The

Trees are Turning colors already.

Another person I haven't mentioned, Just came To mind. Her name was Bessie FarToLotte. She always wore Sunglasses and Talked on her cell phones. She always was whiney, bossy, gassy, and Took forever To do a run.

And Then there's dispatch. I don't know if I've mentioned him or not, but I'll call him CLem. I Think he's from South Boston. He's fun To Talk with.

We were at a stop
today, and some old lady
came up to the truck, wanting
to ask me something. But
she wanted me to <u>roll the</u>
<u>window down!</u> Well, rolling
the window down isn't going
to happen, so I played like
I couldn't hear what she
was saying. And she gave up
trying to talk to me.

This week we were coming
back to base from a run,
and we got hammered by
heavy rain. And so it goes
at hillbilly armored inc.

one time on old run 6,
we stopped some place to get
something to eat. IT was
winter, and The messenger
wanted some hot chocolate
but didn't have any money
To buy it. So I went inside
after The messenger came
up front. I asked the
messenger what size drink
he wanted, and he said The
biggest They have. I came
back with my breakfast and
a great big value sized cup
of hot chocolate for the
messenger. That cup was so
big they had To ring it up
Twice! The messenger looked

at it, and said he'd be bouncing
off The walls if he drank it
all. I don't know how much
of it he drank, but we got
finished, with The run early
That day. That messengers name
will be changed TO CLem.

on The Same run 6, but a
different day, something else
happened. I stopped and got
my breakfast with a Large
sweet iced tea. I tied The
drink to The dashboard of the
truck, with a rubberband so
I could drive The Truck To
The next Stop. But on The
way, I had To Stop at a red

Light going up a hill, when
the light turned green, and we
started moving up the hill, the
cup of tea came out of the
place where it was tied up,
and exploded on the floor,
of the truck. I was mad as
hell, because it was a quart sized
cup, and I didn't have any money
for another drink. I guess
just one rubberband isn't enough
to hold a big drink like that.
I used every napkin and paper
towel I had, to clean that
mess up.

more recently Though, I was flashed by a woman. Now, I'm not complainin but I Just Thought I'd put it in the book. This woman came out of the store that I was parked in front of, and got in her car. I Just happened to glance around, and she pulled her boots out and flashed me with them! I have no idea who she was, but I Look at pickup Trucks differently now.

Here's another old run 23 flashback. We were going back to Atlanta, and I noticed one of the mirrors was

Starting to wiggle and flap
in the wind. The mounts holding
the mirror must have had
metal fatigue, because all of
a sudden the mirror just
dropped off the truck. I did
a double take, when that
happened and said "well, there
goes the mirror!". The guard
riding shotgun got a good
laugh out of it, and we went
back to Atlanta and got it
replaced.

This Friday, I'll be back at
the airport again. I have no
idea what I'll be doing next
week, but I'll find out Friday.

While I'm waiting for another
memory to come along, I
guess I better start gearing
this thing down a bit.
Everything in this book really
did happen, but the names
have been changed and some
details were left out on
purpose, to cover my ass. And
because I didn't want hillbilly
armored coming to me bitching,
about giving away company
secrets. Besides, they don't
have any secrets that are
worth a shit anyway. Believe
it or not, I never know how
much money is on the truck.
And I also don't care.

The end of the book is
getting close, so I guess
I'll go ahead and keep writing
until its done.

I know a lot of people
will think this book is
disjointed, because of the
way its written. IT does
jump around a lot, I admit
that. And some other people
will think that a lot of
detail was left out. That's
also true. But too much
detail, is boring, and boring
books don't sell very well.
IT jumps around a lot,
because thats the way

The memories and stories
came to me. There isn't any
chronological order to any of
it, because I can't remember
the order that they happened
in. Also, it's more fun to
not really know, what you'll
find on the next page.

The real reason I wrote
this wonderful work of
literary art is simple.
I wanted to help people
understand why armored trucks
do what they do. You might
not always understand, but
there's a reason for everything
you see us doing. It's just

That we can't stop to explain
it. The bad guys are out
there, and we don't know
who they are, or where they
are. So that's, why I wrote
hillbilly armored inc.

Another reason, why so much
detail was left out is,
I wanted you to use your
imagination to get more out
of the stories and memories.
It's been a wild ride for
me in the trucks, I've driven.
No two days are ever the
same. If I was to put
the pen down now, and stop
writing I would be happy,

but I still have Some
pages To go before I'm done.

Today is halloween, and The
only Strange Thing Thats
happened, is That nothing Strange
has happened ...... yet!
I've seen Some people out
Trick or Treating, and I can't
figure out if They're dressed
for halloween, or if That's The
way They dress everyday.
Anyway, This Should be another
good week.

OK, you remember cleb That
Took otis's place because otis
doesn't work here anymore? well,

Cleb wants me to write a chapter about him in this book. But I told Cleb that there ain't any chapters in this book. I think I'll tell Cleb to hold his breath, while Looking for his chapter, and see how Long it takes for him to pass out.

I think tomorrow will be a long day. I'm going to be on a North Georgia run. It's the new run 23. Let me punch it up on the hillbilly gps, real quick.

The new run 23 according
to The hillbilly GPS Thing.

The new run 23

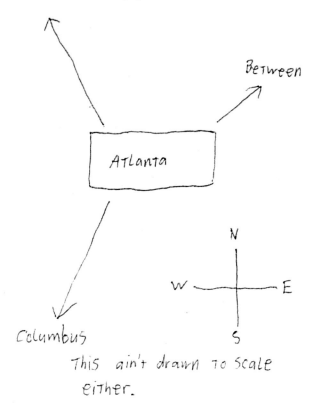

Between

Atlanta

N
W — — E
S

Columbus

This ain't drawn to scale
either.

Isn't hillbilly GPS, wonderful?
IT makes getting LOST So
much easier.

IT's time to go to The
next Stop.

This week is Turning out
To be a good week. ThankSgiving
is JuST a few dayS away,
and The nuts are already on
The road. I'll be glad if They
all go in The Same direction!

I'm on The columbus run,
Tomorrow with a Three day
weekend coming.

I Think I'm going to have
to finish This by writing
Stuff, as it happens because
the memories are getting
farther apart. My next
vacation isn't far away,
and I'm hoping it's going to
be a good one.

For some reason, there's bees
buzzing around The Truck.
I'm on The Columbus run
Today, and it's another day
at hillbilly armored inc.
IT Looks Like we might
get some rain either tonight
or tomorrow.

It's been another day of people, Looking at me Like it's my fault They don't have a brain. And Lots of others Talking and Texting on Their phones while They're driving. I guess They'll never Learn.

I'll be back on The cleanout run Tomorrow. It's about Time To go back To base.

There's another person I'll mention. His name will be cleb. Now cleb is a good person, but I swear on a bucket of dollars, That

he has polar bear blood
in him. In the winter,
I've seen him come to work
in short pants, and a short
sleeve shirt like it's summer.
And still he doesn't get
cold. Anyway, I'm on at least
four different runs this
next week.

I'm on the columbus run
today, and I saw a sign
that's just to crazy to make
up. It said, "funeral
insurance. No exam required."
It was in the middle of
nowhere, like all of the
crazy stuff I see.

I never thought I'd see
a sign like that. There
wasn't much to it, because
the only other thing on it
was a telephone number.
I wonder how many people
buy funeral insurance, with
the idea that they <u>just might</u>
live long enough to use it?
Who would underwrite that
kind of stuff? I don't know
but maybe, "Rigor mortis
funeral insurance agency, Lucky
Stiff President."

It looks like rain in a
little while here. But we
should be done with the run

before it starts.

There's some thing else that happened in the early 90's. Some body that I'll call Clem was going to a bank inside a bigger building, got shot just outside the door of The Stop. The guy that shot Clem, was wearing a Three piece Suit. And Clem got shot in The Left Shoulder. Because of The way The bullet broke up, The doctors couldn't take it out, So Clem carried That bullet in his Shoulder for The rest of his Life, Clem died in 2010.

Also, somebody I'll call Billybob, got shot just outside a store. Billybob was coming back out to the truck, when somebody came up and shot him at almost point blank range with a shotgun. The police chased the bad guy, and killed him because the bad guy tried to kill the police. The money was recovered and as far as I can tell, Billybob is still alive. This also happened in the early 90's.

Today is a good day, but it's been raining and I have a serious case of gas, I have the silent but deadly farts.

The guy that drives the
clean out run wants his name
in this book to be sleep dog.
He was in the marines a long
time ago. He's also in a
motorcycle club. The messenger's
name will be Goober. Goober
is also a good friend, along
with a lot of others I talked
about.

Well, today is coming to an
end and so is this book.
Tomorrow is another day at
hillbilly armored inc., with the
holidays just about here.
And there'll be more road
kills, fartin in the truck,

hold ups, and everything else.
I wrote This crazy book to
entertain, and educate people
about my Job driving armored
Trucks. Please give all Truck
drivers a break. I hope you
enJoyed reading This and got
SomeThing out of iT.
I better get going now,
because This page iS running
out. Drive Safe, be careful,
and have a good Life.
Thanks for visiting
Hillbilly armored inc., I'm
DanieL R Poncinie. I finished
writing This on 11/17/11.

The End